NOTED NAMES FOR BELGIAN BABY BOYS AND GIRLS

AHSRAH AYIR

Contents

Contents

Preface

Experts say that the name has a great impact on the life of a human being, so the name should be meaningful. Therefore, while naming a child, parents insist that the name be auspicious and reflect the personality of the child well. According to the principles of naming, it is concluded that the name has a special relationship with our behavior. Names in our lives not only give information about our personality, but they are also an important part of our future.

If seen, the first identity of a child is his or her name, which remains associated with him or her throughout his or her life. There are many things to keep in mind while naming a child, such as family customs, traditions, social rules, and many more. All these aspects should be considered while choosing a name. The name should be chosen so that it is easy to pronounce as well as meaningful.

In many places, you can guess the religion of the child by his name. By the way, in modern times, people do not give much importance to religions, etc. when naming. All they need is a catchy and easy name for their babies. Despite all these things, it is difficult for any parent to name a child because every parent wants their child's name to be the most different and attractive.

Generally, a baby should be named in such a way that it is sweet and beautiful to hear. Too difficult a name can sometimes cause trouble for that child in the future. Often, there are mistakes in the documents made while writing difficult names, which have to be circulated to the government offices to correct them, and many problems have to be faced. So the name should be something that is beautiful as well as easy to speak and write. This will save you and your baby from many problems.

If you take care of the things mentioned here, then you will be able to choose the best name for your baby.

Keep in mind that trendy names should be avoided. Choose a simple name that has a deep message or meaning hidden in it. Nowadays, the trend of naming such names has increased a lot. At the same time, it is believed that the meaning of the name also affects the nature of people. So, whatever name you give, its meaning will affect the behaviour of your child. Having the name for too long can upset the child. Give names that are easy to pronounce. The spelling of the name should also be easy.

In the end, we can say that naming babies is a very important and difficult task. Even before the birth of the child, parents spend a lot of time thinking about the name of the child, and sometimes even after the birth of the child, no name is finalized. In such a situation, keeping in mind the above-mentioned tips, you can give the right name to your child, and this book can prove to be helpful in this. It consists of alphabetically chosen and meaningful names for your baby. So it can become a useful and collectible book for you, your family, and your friends.

—Author

I
Belgian Baby Names—A

Adalgiso—(m)—gently born hostage

Adalheida—(f)—sweet, gently born

Adalric—(m)—gently born friend

Adela—(f)—easeful, pleasing, gently born

Adele—(f)—pleasurable, delicious, illumination, beacon, lightness

Adelgonde—(f)—gently born female, woman, lady, dame

Adelhard—(m)—resolute

Adelia—(f)—of the nobility, gently born

Adelisa—(f)—of the nobility, gently born

Adelynn—(f)—good humour

Adie—(f)—gently born, kind

Adlar—(m)—eagle

Agatha—(f)—good

Agathe—(f)—kind natured female, woman, lady, dame

Agneta—(f)—holy, pure, sanctified, pious, solemn, chaste

Ahren—(m)—eagle

Aimee—(f)—dear, darling, sweetheart

Alain—(m)—harmony, stone, gently born, fair, handsome

Alair—(f)—glad, cheery, complacent, hilarious, jolly

Alarice—(f)—all ruler

Alarick—(m)—gently born leader

Alder—(m)— the name of the tree

Aldona—(f)—ancient, pristine, old, antiquated, primitive

Alessandro—(m)—defender of man

Alex—(m)—defender of humanity

Alexander—(m)—patron, guardian, custodian, protector, trustee, promoter

Alexandra—(f)—feminine of alexander, defender of humanity

Alexandrine—(f)—protector, defender, keeper, savior, life saver, intercessor of humanity

Alexis—(m)—helper, defender, variant of alexander

Alfons—(m)—gently born estate, eager

Alice—(f)—gently born, truth, of the nobility

Alicia—(f)—of gently born

Alicia—(f)—sweet

Aline—(f)—fair, good-looking

Alison—(f)—gently born, truth

Aliz—(f)—gently born, truth

Ally—(f)—gently born, truth

Aloisia—(f)—noted, celebrated, shining, well-known, well-born fighting

Aloysius—(m)—warrior

Alphonse—(m)—gently born estate, eager

Alvar—(f)— an army of elves

Alyda—(f)—ancient, pristine, old, antiquated, primitive, archaic

Amalasand—(f)—industrious

Amara—(f)—everlasting, endless, infinitude, interminable

Amaury—(m)— the name of count

Amber—(f)—jewel name

Amdt—(m)—one with the power of an eagle

Amey—(m)—eagle

Amina—(f)—honest, upright, sincere, conscientious, straightforward

Amy—(f)—dearly affection, dearness, devotion, dear, darling, sweetheart

An—(f)—gracious, sweet and despiteful, smart, sardonic, sad

Anaïs—(f)—gracious, merciful

Andreas—(m)— a german form of andrew

Andy—(m)—diminutive of andrew, manly

Angela—(f)—angel, apostle

Angeletta—(f)—little angel, apostle, girl, gal, daughter, damsel, affection

Angelique—(f)—like an angel, apostle

Angie—(f)—angel, an apostle of wine

Anique—(f)— favour, graciousness, indulgence, favour

Anita—(f)—gracious, sweet and despiteful, sardonic, sad

Anja—(f)—dearness, devotion

Anke—(f)—dutch form of anne

Ann—(f)— favour, graciousness, indulgence

Anna—(f)—gracious, sweet and despiteful, sardonic, sad

Anne—(f)—charming, gracious

Anneleen—(f)—charming, gracious

Annelies—(f)—charming, gracious

Annemie—(f)—despiteful, swart, sardonic favour, graciousness, indulgence

Annie—(f)—the traditional folk song annie laurie

Anouck—(f)—gracious, affection, dearness, devotion, mashly

Anouk—(f)—favor, favor, graciousness, indulgence

Anthony—(m)—flower

Apollina—(f)—gift, present, keepsake, fairing, bounty, prize from apollo

Apsel—(m)—father of serenity, calm, calmness, stillness, silence

Arabel—(f)—pretty, affection, dearness, devotion, handsome, scenic

Arcene—(f)—silvery

Aric—(m)—gently born leader

Arlise—(f)—deity's oath

Arnaud—(m)—eagle, powerful

Arne—(m)—he who reigns as an eagle

Arno—(m)—he who reigns as an eagle

Arnout—(m)—he who reigns as an eagle

Arthur—(m)—gently born, courageous, noted, celebrated, shining, well-known, well-born bearer

Arvin—(m)—friend to all

Ashley—(f)—lives in the ash tree grove

Astrid—(f)—divine, providential, supernal beauty

Audrey—(f)—variant of etheldreda

Audrick—(m)—gently born friend

Avaset—(f)—bird, birth

Aveline—(f)—nut

Axel—(m)—my father is serenity, calm, calmness, stillness, silence

Axelle—(f)—my father is serenity, calm, calmness, stillness, silence

Azure—(f)—sky-blue

II
Belgian Baby Names—B

Bailey—(m)—bailiff, fortification, able

Baldric—(m)—valiant, gallant, heroic, daring, valorous

Bamard—(m)—valiant, gallant, heroic, daring, valorous as bear

Barbara—(f)—savage, wild

Bari—(m)—spear thrower, marksman

Barny—(m)—from the name bernard

Barrie—(m)—spear thrower, marksman

Bart—(m)—radiant, vivid, orient, splendent, flamboyant, shiny

Bartlett—(m)—farmer, peasant, husbandman, agriculturist, agriculturalist, swain

Bas—(m)—majestic

Bayard—(m)—a bay horse

Baylor—(m)—bailiff, fortification, able

Baz—(m)—the unwavering protector, defender, keeper, saviour, life saver, intercessor

Beall—(m)—handsome

Beauvais—(m)—one belonging to beauvais, from beauvais

Bebe—(m)—baby

Belva—(f)—pretty, affection, dearness, devotion, handsome, scenic, grace

Bem—(m)—bear

Ben—(m)—son of happiness

Benjamin—(m)—son of happiness

Berangaria—(f)—name of princess

Berdine—(f)—noble, kingly, supreme, statuesque

Bergen—(m)—mountain dweller

Bernadete—(f)—valiant, gallant, heroic, daring, valorous as bear

Bernardyn—(m)—valiant, gallant, heroic, daring, valorous as bear

Berniss—(f)—the one who brings victory, conquest, success

Bert—(m)—pretty, affection, dearness, devotion, handsome, scenic

Berthe—(f)—radiant, vivid, orient, splendent, flamboyant

Berthold—(m)—radiant, vivid, orient, splendent, flamboyant ruler

Bertl—(m)—one who is noted, celebrated, shining, well-known, well-born for nobility

Bertrand—(m)—intelligent, noble, kingly, supreme, statuesque raven

Bess—(f)—deity's oath

Beth—(f)—deity's oath

Betty—(f)—deity has sworn

Bieke—(f)—bend, bow

Birger—(m)—deliverance, emancipation, extrication, releasement, rescue, uplift

Birgit—(f)—variation of the name bridget

Bjorn—(m)—bear

Blaisdell—(m)— a person who lisps, stutters

Blanche—(f)—white, shining

Blaz—(m)—unwavering protector, defender, keeper, savior, life saver, intercessor

Blondell—(f)—fair-haired, blonde

Bluma—(f)—flower, bloom

Bo—(f)—respected, regarded highly

Bo—(m)—diminutive of beauregard, respected, regarded highly

Bob—(m)—pretty, affection, dearness, devotion, handsome, scenic, gracely by fame

Bourke—(m)—birch tree

Bram—(m)—father of many nations

Brandy—(f)—brandy drink

Branko—(m)— armour, defence

Brann—(f)—brandy drink

Brecht—(m)—pretty, affection, dearness, devotion, handsome, scenic

Bren—(m)—flame, blaze

Brent—(m)—high place, steep hill, burnt

Briand—(m)—powerful, strong, energetic, sledgehammer, swinging, driving, hill

Brigham—(m)—soldier, constable, man, effective, uhlan, adventurer

Brigitte—(f)—variant of bridget, strength

Britt—(f)—brit

Bronson—(m)—brown's son

Bruce—(m)—thick brush

Brune—(f)—of the black, dark, somber, dusky, unlit, ebon hair

Brunhilde—(f)—battle, fight, fighting, war, action, struggle armor

Bryan—(m)—high, gently born

Brys—(m)—from brys

Burdett—(m)—surname

Burhardt—(m)—powerful, strong, energetic, sledgehammer

III

Belgian Baby Names—C

Camille—(f)—noted, celebrated, shining, well-known, well-born

Camillei—(f)—free, independent, unoccupied, quit, devoid-born, highborn, gentle

Capucina—(f)—cape

Cara—(f)—powerful, strong, energetic, driving

Carina—(f)—holy, pure, sanctified, pious, solemn, chaste

Carine—(f)—holy, pure, sanctified, pious, solemn, chaste

Carl—(m)—powerful, strong, energetic, sledgehammer, swinging, driving, manly

Carlijn—(f)—free, independent, unoccupied, quit, devoid man

Carlin—(m)—man

Carlo—(m)—non-gently born free, independent, unoccupied, quit

Carly—(f)—powerful, strong, energetic, driving, melody, song

Caro—(f)—feminine variant of charles, manly

Caroline—(f)—means the same as guy

Carolyn—(f)—powerful, energetic, driving, melody, song

Cary—(f)—powerful, strong, energetic, driving, melody, song

Case—(m)—chest

Caspar—(m)—royal, aristocratical, majestical

Cedric—(m)—bounty-pattern

Celesse—(f)—heavenly

Celestiel—(f)—heavenly

Celine—(f)—divine, providential, supernal

Cerise—(f)—cherry, cherry red

Chan—(m)—candle maker

Chane—(m)—oak-hearted

Chanler—(m)—candle maker

Channel—(f)—channel

Chantal—(f)—singer, song

Chantell—(f)—singer, vocalist, chanter, chorine, songster, melodist

Chantelle—(f)—singer, vocalist, chanter, chorine, songster, melodist

Charles—(m)—powerful, strong, energetic, sledgehammer, driving, manly

Charlotte—(f)—tiny and feminine

Chaunce—(m)—fortune, gamble

Cherrie—(f)—dear, darling, sweetheart, dear, darling

Cheryle—(f)—dear, darling, sweetheart, dear, darling

Cheval—(m)—horseman, knight

Cheval—(m)—knight, horseman and rider

Chevalier—(m)—horseman, knight

Chiana—(f)—algonquian tribe, place name

Chiara—(f)—radiant, vivid, orient, splendent, flamboyant, shining, clear

Chloris—(f)—pale

Choncey—(m)—fortune, gamble

Chris—(m)—anointed

Chriselda—(f)—powerful, strong, energetic, sledgehammer, driving

Christian—(m)—anointed

Christine—(f)—anointed

Christof—(m)— a variant of christopher

Christophe—(m)— a variant of christopher

Ciel—(f)—shield, scholar

Ciel—(m)—shield, scholar

Cindy—(f)—dimunitive of cynthia, lucinda, cinderella

Clara—(f)—radiant, vivid, orient, splendent, flamboyant, shiny, glossy

Clarita—(f)—radiant, vivid, orient, splendent, flamboyant, shining, clear

Claudia—(f)—lame

Claudine—(f)—lame

Clayborne—(f)—adhere, mortal

Coletta—(f)—victorious

Colette—(f)—necklace, public, people, demos, folk, conquest, success

Colin—(m)— a variant of nicholas, public, people, demos, folk

Con—(m)—valiant, gallant, heroic, daring, valorous counsel, wise

Conny—(f)—powerful, strong, energetic, sledgehammer

Conradin—(m)—honest advisor

Conradina—(f)—valiant, gallant, heroic, daring, valorous

Corben—(m)—raven-haired

Corbett—(m)—raven, black hair

Cort—(m)—valiant, gallant, heroic, daring, valorous counsel, wise

Corwan—(m)—raven, black hair

Courtland—(m)—court attendant

Courtnay—(m)—from the court

Curt—(m)—courteous

Cynthia—(f)—from kinthos

IV
Belgian Baby Names—D

Daan—(m)—my judge is a deity

Dagmar—(f)—serenity, calm, calmness, stillness, silence

Dagobert—(m)—shining sun

Daisy—(f)—day's eye, from the old english

Dame—(f)—lady

Damien—(m)—one who tames

Daniel—(m)—deity is my judge

Danny—(m)—deity is my judge

Daphne—(f)—victory, conquest, success

Darcel—(f)—black, dark, somber, dusky, unlit, ebon

Darcey—(f)—black, dark, somber, dusky, unlit, ebon

Darcio—(m)—black, dark, somber, dusky, unlit, ebon, from arcy

Dareau—(m)—dearly affection, dearness, devotion, open

Dareau—(m)—one who is dearly affection, dearness, devotion, open

Dario—(m)—to maintain

Darroll—(m)—dearly affection, dearness, devotion, open

Davet—(m)—dear, darling, sweetheart

David—(m)—darling, dear, darling, sweetheart

Davy—(m)—dear, darling, sweetheart, friend

Deborah—(f)—bee

Deiter—(m)— an army of the public, people, demos, folk, many

Delaine—(m)—from the elder tree grove

Delancy—(m)—from the elder tree grove

Delma—(f)—gently born protector, defender, keeper, savior, life saver, intercessor

Delmer—(m)—sailor, navigator, handyman, seaman, mariner, seafarer

Delphine—(f)—dolphin

Deman—(m)—pet, tamed, domestic, tame, home

Dennet—(m)—named for saint denys

Dennis—(m)—fertility

Denyse—(f)—of dionysus

Deon—(m)—of dionysus

Derrall—(m)—dearly affection, dearness, devotion, open

Derrick—(m)—gift, present, keepsake, fairing, bounty

Desarae—(f)—the one desired by everyone

Desirae—(f)—long hoped for, desired

Deston—(m)—destiny

Destry—(m)—surname

Devana—(f)—divine, providential, supernal

Deverel—(m)—place name

Deverell—(m)—place name

Devonna—(f)—divine, providential, supernal

Devonne—(f)—divine, providential, supernal

Di—(f)—divine, providential, supernal

Diamanta—(f)—like diamond

Diane—(f)—divine, providential, supernal

Diannah—(f)—divine, providential, supernal

Dickie—(m)—powerful ruler

Didier—(m)—desire, incline, volition, inclination, intent, readiness

Diede—(m)—protector, defender, keeper, saviour, life saver, intercessor of the public

Diederich—(m)—public, people, demos, folk

Diederik—(m)—ruler, powerful

Dieter—(m)— an army of the public, people, demos, folk, many

Dietger—(m)— the spear of the public, people, demos, folk, many

Dietlinde—(f)—unknown

Dietz—(m)—public, people, demos, folk

Dilan—(m)—like a lion

Dimitri—(m)—son of demeter

Dina—(f)—rated

Dion—(m)—of dionysus

Dirk—(m)—powerful among the public, people, demos, folk, many

Domenique—(f)—of the lord

Dominique—(m)—of the lord

Doreen—(f)—golden, yellow

Dorien—(f)—young and handsome

Dries—(m)—manlike, manly, valiant, gallant, heroic, daring, valorous

Drugi—(m)—powerful, strong, energetic, sledgehammer, driving

Dylan—(m)—son of the wave, born near the sea, influence

V

Belgian Baby Names—E

Eagan—(m)—fiery, forceful

Eberhardt—(m)—powerful, strong, energetic, sledgehammer, driving aboard

Eckerd—(m)—sacred

Edda—(f)—vigorous battle, fight, fighting, war, action, struggle maiden

Eddy—(m)—wealth, patron, guardian, custodian, protector, trustee, promoter of the property

Eden—(m)—beacon, lightness, luminosity, radiance

Edgarton—(m)—prosperous warrior

Edgerton—(m)—prosperous warrior

Edith—(f)—happy warfare, spoils of war

Edward—(m)—powerful, strong, energetic, sledgehammer

Edwin—(m)—rich friend

Eginhardt—(m)—powerful, strong, energetic, sledgehammer, driving with a sword

Elayna—(f)—shining illumination, beacon, lightness, luminosity, radiance

Elayne—(f)—illumination, beacon, lightness, luminosity, radiance

Elbert—(m)—radiant, vivid, orient, splendent, flamboyant, noted, celebrated, shining, well-known

Eldwin—(m)— an old friend

Elias—(m)—yahweh is my deity

Elicia—(f)—devoted to deity

Elien—(f)—torch, the radiant

Eline—(f)—torch, the shining, brilliant

Elisa—(f)—consecrated to deity

Elise—(f)—deity has sworn

Elisha—(f)—devoted to deity

Elita—(f)—chosen

Elizabeth—(f)—deity's oath

Elka—(f)—gently born, truth

Elke—(f)—of gently born

Ellaine—(f)—beacon, lightness, luminosity, radiance

Ellen—(f)—shining, illumination, beacon, lightness, luminosity

Els—(f)—deity has sworn

Elsbeth—(f)—deity's oath

Elsie—(f)—consecrated to deity

Emelia—(f)—industrious, eager

Emera—(f)—industrious leader

Emest—(m)—serious

Emiel—(m)—gentle, friendly, competitor

Emile—(m)—gentle, friendly, contestant

Emilie—(f)—gentle, friendly, contestant

Emily—(f)—rival

Emma—(f)—great great

Emmeline—(f)—hardworking

Emmy—(f)—great, great

Emmylou—(f)—whole, complete

Emory—(m)—leader

Engleberta—(f)—radiant, vivid, orient, splendent, flamboyant angel, apostle

Enno—(m)—powerful, strong, energetic, sledgehammer, driving with a sword

Erchanhardt—(m)—sacred

Eric—(m)—ruler of the law

Erik—(m)—ruler of the law

Erma—(f)—complete war deity

Ernest—(m)—earnest, vigorous

Ernesta—(f)—earnest, vigorous

Ernst—(m)—earnest, vigorous

Erwin—(m)—boar friend, sea friend

Estee—(f)—star

Estelle—(f)—star

Esther—(f)—star

Etta—(f)—little one

Eva—(f)—life, living one

Evelien—(f)—the life giving

Eveline—(f)—variant of evelyn, hazelnut

Everett—(m)—powerful, strong, energetic, sledgehammer, driving wild boar

Evi—(f)—the life giving

Evrard—(m)—powerful, strong, energetic, sledgehammer

Evy—(f)—the life giving

VI

Belgian Baby Names—F

Farahilde—(f)— travelling, battle, fight, fighting, war, action, struggle

Faunia—(f)—fawn

Fawna—(f)—young deer

Fayanna—(f)—trust, belief, faith, affiance, assurance, credence, sureness

Faye—(f)—belief, faith, affiance, assurance, credence, sureness, trust

Fayette—(f)—little fairy

Febe—(f)—radiant, vivid, orient, splendent, flamboyant, shining

Felicia—(f)—great happiness

Felien—(f)—fruitful, happy, auspicious, blessed, energetic, happy

Felisberta—(f)—an intelligent and wise female, woman, lady, dame

Felix—(m)—pleased, happy, allegro, bean fed, blissful, blithesome

Femke—(f)—girl, gal, daughter, damsel

Ferd—(m)—courageous traveller

Ferdinand—(m)—adventurer

Fernand—(m)— a variant of ferdinand, valiant, gallant, heroic, daring, valorous traveller

Ferre—(m)—security, courageous protector, defender, keeper, saviour, life saver, intercessor

Fien—(f)—added

Filip—(m)—horses friend

Finn—(m)—fair, mythology

Fitz—(m)—son

Fitzpatrick—(m)—son of patrick

Florian—(m)—bloom

Florrie—(f)—flower

Fons—(m)—willing, subservient

Fontane—(m)—fountain

Fontayne—(m)—fountain

Fortune—(m)—lucky

Francene—(f)—free, independent, unoccupied, quit, devoid

Frances—(f)—free, independent, unoccupied, quit, devoid

Franci—(m)—free, independent, unoccupied, devoid

Francis—(m)—from france, free, independent, unoccupied, quit, devoid

Frank—(m)—frenchman, free, independent, unoccupied, quit, devoid one

Franklin—(m)—free, independent, unoccupied, quit, devoid man

Franky—(m)—free, independent, unoccupied, quit, devoid

Frans—(m)—variant of franz, frenchman

Fraser—(m)—strawberry

Fred—(m)—serenity, calm, calmness, stillness, silenceful ruler

Freddy—(m)—serenity, calm, calmness, stillness, silenceful ruler

Frederic—(m)—powerful protector, defender, keeper, savior, life saver

Frederica—(f)—serenity, calm, calmness, stillness, silenceful ruler

Frederick—(m)—pacific

Frederik—(m)—defender, keeper, savior, life saver, intercessor

Fredricka—(f)—serenity, calm, calmness, stillness, silenceful ruler

Fremont—(m)—gently born protector, defender, keeper

Frieda—(f)—serenity, calm, calmness, stillness, silence, joy

VII
Belgian Baby Names—G

Gaetan—(m)—fom gaete

Galatee—(f)—white

Galiana—(f)—supreme one

Gard—(m)—keeper of the garden

Garlan—(m)—wreath, prize

Garland—(f)—crowned in victory, conquest, success

Garnell—(m)—keeper of grain

Garon—(m)—guards, patron, guardian, custodian, protector, trustee, promoter

Garrey—(m)—spear

Garrin—(m)—patron, guardian, custodian, protector, trustee, promoter

Garron—(m)—guards, patron, guardian, custodian, protector, trustee

Gascon—(m)—from gascony, one who belongs to gascony

Gauthier—(m)—powerful ruler

Gaye—(m)—merry, glad, rapt, happy, delighted, immersed

Geert—(m)—powerful, strong, energetic, sledgehammer, driving with the spear

Geneva—(f)—of the race of women, white wave

Genevia—(f)—juniper berry

Genevie—(f)—of the race of women

Genivee—(f)—of the race of women

Geoff—(m)—serenity, calm, calmness, stillness, silenceful

Geoffrey—(m)—divine, providential, supernal serenity, calm, calmness, stillness, silence

Geoffrey—(m)—serenity, calm, calmness, stillness, silence of deity

Georges—(m)—farmer, peasant, husbandman, agriculturist, agriculturalist, swain

Georgine—(f)—farmer, peasant, husbandman, agriculturist, agriculturalist, swain

Gerald—(m)—spear warrior

Gerda—(f)— defence, protection, defensive, guard, immunity, parry

Gerda—(f)—powerful, strong, energetic, sledgehammer, swinging

Gerdie—(f)—protected, she who is protected by deity

Geron—(m)—guards, patron, guardian, custodian, protector, trustee, promoter

Gerrard—(m)—spear powerful, strong, energetic, sledgehammer, driving

Gerrit—(m)—powerful, strong, energetic, sledgehammer, driving with the spear

Gert—(m)—powerful, strong, energetic, sledgehammer, driving with the spear

Gilles—(m)—small goat

Gino—(m)—noted, celebrated, shining, well-known, well-born

Gisela—(f)—pledge, oath

Gitte—(f)— a variation of the name bridget

Glenn—(m)—valley, canyon, basin, vale, purgatory, gulch

Godelief—(m)—affection, dearness, devotion, mashd by the deitys, good life

Godelieve—(f)—deity's affection, dearness, devotion, mash

Gofried—(m)—serenity, calm, calmness, stillness, silenceful deity

Gregory—(m)—on the watch

Greta—(f)—pearl

Gricelda—(f)—gray, gray-haired

Griet—(f)—pearl

Griswold—(m)—from the gray forest, wood, bush

Grizelda—(f)—endless patience

Gudruna—(f)—one with divine, providential, supernal knowledge

Guido—(m)—wood, forest, wood, bush, forest, wood, bush

Guy—(m)—wood, forest, wood, bush, forest, wood, bush

VIII

Belgian Baby Names—H

Hadu—(f)—vigorous battle, fight, fighting, war, action, struggle maiden

Hagen—(m)—not available

Halfrida—(f)—serenity, calm, calmness, stillness, silenceful heroine

Hank—(m)—ruler of an estate

Hannah—(f)— favour, graciousness, indulgence of deity

Hanne—(f)—deity is gracious

Hannelore—(f)—deity is gracious

Hannes—(m)—yahweh is gracious

Harbin—(m)—noted, celebrated, shining, well-known, well-born warrior

Harimann—(m)—protective

Harti—(m)—daring

Hedvige—(f)—fighter, refuge in battle, fight, fighting, war, action

Hedwig—(f)—refuge in battle, fight, fighting, war, action, struggle

Hedy—(f)—strife

Heidi—(f)—of gently born

Helaine—(f)—radiant, vivid, orient, splendent, flamboyant one, most pretty, affection

Helena—(f)—torch, the radiant

Helmutt—(m)—valiant, gallant, heroic, daring, valorous

Henri—(m)—ruler king

Henriella—(f)—ruler of the house, female, woman, lady, the lady who rules the house

Herbst—(m)—soldier, constable, man, effective, uhlan, adventurer

Herman—(m)—warrior

Herta—(f)—of the earth

Hervé—(m)—battle, fight, fighting, war, action, struggle

Hettie—(f)—rules her household

Hewlitt—(m)—little

Hilde—(f)—battle, fight, fighting, war, action, struggle maid,

Hilde—(f)—gently born

Hildimar—(f)—one who is noble, kingly, supreme, statuesque, noble, kingly, supreme, statuesque

Hobbard—(m)—high, radiant, vivid, orient, splendent, flamboyant

Holle—(f)—dear, darling, sweetheart, dear, darling, sweetheart of everyone

Hugo—(m)—thinking mind, wise

Hulbart—(m)—favor, graciousness

Hulde—(f)—dear, darling, sweetheart, dear to everyone

Hunfried—(m)—serenity, calm, calmness, stillness

IX

Belgian Baby Names—I

Ida—(f)—female, woman, lady who is hardworking

Idas—(m)—an argonaut

Idna—(f)—active, one who is active and agile

Idonia—(f)—industrious and fruitful

Ignace—(m)—fiery, fierce, radical, acrimonious, hot, forceful

Ikram—(f)—honour, respect

Ilana—(f)—torch, the radiant, pretty, affection, dearness, devotion, mashly

Ilias—(m)—jehovah is deity

Ilke—(f)—hard at work

Ilse—(f)—deity has sworn

Imke—(f)—whole, comprehensive

Ine—(f)—clean, holy, pure, sanctified, pious, solemn, chaste

Ines—(f)—meek, chaste, variant of agnes

Inge—(f)—alternative name for the nordic deity freyr

Ingrid—(f)—alternative name for the nordic deity freyr

Inne—(f)—clean, holy, pure, sanctified, pious, solemn, chaste

Iolanthe—(f)—violet

Iris—(f)—colorful, rainbow

Irmigard—(f)—war deitydess

Isabeau—(f)—dedicated to deity

Isabel—(f)—deity's oath

Isabelle—(f)—dedicated to deity

Isolda—(f)—the ruler of ice

Ivan—(m)—yahweh is gracious

Ivo—(m)—archer

X
Belgian Baby Names—J

Jacquelynne—(f)—supplanter, variation of jacqueline

Jacquenette—(f)—little jacques

Jacques—(m)—supplanter

Jade—(f)—the name of the semi-precious stone

Jakobe—(f)—supplanter

Jakoh—(m)—supplanter

Jan—(m)—deity is merciful

Jana—(f)—derived word

Janez—(m)—deity's gracious gift, present, keepsake, fairing, bounty, prize

Janne—(f)—deity is gracious

Jaquelin—(f)—supplanter

Jarman—(m)—from germany, bud

Jarne—(m)—exalted of the lord

Jarno—(m)—fancy name

Jaro—(m)—yahweh founds

Jasmine—(f)—jasmine blossom

Jasmyne—(f)—flower name

Jasper—(m)—treasurer

Jay—(m)—blue jay

Jeanette—(f)—little jean

Jeanice—(f)—deity is merciful

Jef—(m)—serenity, calm, calmness, stillness, silence of deity

Jeffrey—(m)—divine, providential, supernal serenity, calm, calmness, stillness, silence

Jelke—(f)—value, payment, retribution, sacrifice

Jelle—(m)—value, payment, retribution, sacrifice

Jeni—(f)—knowledge

Jennifer—(f)—fruitful

Jenny—(f)—fruitful

Jens—(m)—deity is gracious

Jente—(m)—deity is gracious

Jeroen—(m)—with holy name

Jesse—(m)—gift, present, keepsake, fairing, bounty, prize

Jessica—(f)—rich, deity beholds

Jessie—(f)—yahweh is

Jill—(f)—child of the deitys

Jo—(m)—yahweh is gracious

Joachim—(m)—yahweh focuses on

Joella—(f)—jehovah is deity

Joeri—(m)—farmer, peasant, husbandman, agriculturist, agriculturalist, swain, husbandman

Johan—(m)—yahweh is gracious

Johnn—(m)—deity is merciful

John-paul—(m)—deity is merciful

Joi—(f)—pleasure, enjoyment, joy, happiness, delight

Joke—(f)—yahweh is gracious

Jolanka—(f)—county

Joleigh—(f)—glad, cheery, complacent, hilarious, jolly, pretty

Jolie—(f)—pretty, affection, dearness, devotion, handsome, scenic, grace

Jolien—(f)—deity is gracious

Jonas—(m)—dove, variant of hebrew jonah

Jonathan—(m)—gift, present, keepsake, fairing, bounty, prize from deity

Joni—(f)—modern feminine of john and jon

Jonn—(m)—deity is merciful

Joppe—(m)—he grabbed the heel, he will protect

Joran—(m)—the fictional character jorel father of superman

Jordon—(m)—to descend, to flow

Jordy—(m)—editor of the earth

Joren—(m)—farmer, peasant, husbandman, agriculturist, agriculturalist, swain

Joris—(m)—editor of the earth

Jorn—(m)—farmer, peasant, husbandman, agriculturist, agriculturalist, swain

Jorne—(m)—appears in friesland

Joshka—(m)—jehovah is generous

Joyce—(f)—glad, cheery, complacent, hilarious, jolly, merry

Joyelle—(f)—pleasure, enjoyment, joy, happiness, delight

Jozef—(m)—may the lord add

Jules—(m)—young, juvenescent, under-age, youthful

Julia—(f)—young, juvenescent, under-age, youthful

Julie—(f)—the young, juvenescent, under-age, youthful

Julien—(m)—jove's child

Julien—(m)—jove's descendant

Juliette—(f)—young, juvenescent, under-age, youthful

Julita—(f)—young, juvenescent, under-age, youthful
Jurgen—(m)—editor of the earth
Justine—(f)—righteous, virtuous, good-natured

XI

Belgian Baby Names—K

Kaat—(f)—clean and holy, pure, sanctified, pious, solemn, chaste

Kaatje—(f)—holy, pure, sanctified, pious, solemn, chaste

Karcsi—(m)—powerful, strong, energetic, sledgehammer, driving, manly

Karel—(m)—means the same as the guy

Karen—(f)—the ever holy, pure, sanctified, pious, solemn, chaste

Karl—(m)—powerful, strong, energetic, sledgehammer, driving, manly

Karleen—(f)—female, lady strength

Karleigh—(f)—female, lady strength

Karlina—(f)—female, lady strength

Karlyn—(m)—powerful, strong, energetic, sledgehammer, driving

Karo—(f)—powerful, strong, energetic, sledgehammer, driving

Karolien—(f)—dude, man, free, independent, unoccupied, quit

Karolina—(f)—petite, feminine

Karri—(f)—energetic, sledgehammer, driving, melody, song

Kathleen—(f)—clean, holy, pure, sanctified, pious, solemn, chaste

Kato—(f)—good judgment

Kato—(m)—good judgment

Katriane—(f)—holy, pure, sanctified, pious, solemn, chaste, innocent

Katrien—(f)—clean and holy, pure, sanctified, pious, solemn, chaste

Katrina—(f)—holy, pure, sanctified, pious, solemn, chaste

Kelian—(m)—fight, cell, strife, small water channel

Kellen—(m)—swamp

Kelly—(f)—war, lively, aggressive

Kelsey—(f)—victory, conquest, success

Ken—(m)—born

Kenji—(m)—intelligent second son, powerful, strong, energetic, sledgehammer

Kenneth—(m)—handsome

Kenny—(m)—diminutive of kenneth, handsome

Kevin—(m)—kind, honest, handsome

Kiara—(f)—clear

Kikka—(f)—mistress of all

Kilian—(m)—fight, cell, strife, small water channel

Killian—(m)—fight, cell, strife, small water channel

Kim—(f)—yahweh focuses on

Kim—(m)—yahweh focuses on

Kimberley—(f)—forest, wood

Kimberly—(f)—forest, wood

Kirsten—(f)—the anointed
Kjell—(m)—helmet
Kobe—(m)—he heel grip
Koen—(m)—honest advisor
Koen—(m)—priest
Konstantin—(m)—steadfast
Kris—(m)—anointed
Kristof—(m)—christ carrier
Kuno—(m)—honest advisor
Kurt—(m)—bold counsel, honest advisor
Kyan—(m)—ancient, old
Kyler—(m)—archer

XII

Belgian Baby Names—L

Lacee—(f)—place name

Laciann—(f)—place name

Lacy—(f)—place name

Lana—(f)—rock

Lancelin—(m)—servant

Lander—(m)—from the grassy plain

Landers—(m)—from the grassy plain

Landmari—(m)—noted, celebrated, shining, well-known, well-born land

Lara—(f)—defense, protection, defensive, guard, immunity

Lars—(m)—the award-winning

Lasalle—(m)—the hall

Laura—(f)—the laurel tree, conquest, success

Laure—(f)—bay leaf

Laurel—(f)—laurel

Lauren—(f)—feminine form of lorin, variant of laurence

Lauren—(f)—laurel

Laurence—(f)—the award-winning

Laurens—(m)—the award-winning

Laverne—(f)—born in the spring

Lee—(m)—the king

Leen—(f)—the radiant, powerful, strong, energetic

Lena—(f)—child of illumination, beacon, lightness, luminosity, radiance

Lennard—(m)—valiant, gallant, heroic, daring, valorous as lion

Lennert—(m)—lion, hard

Leo—(m)—lion-hearted

Leodegrance—(m)—lion

Leon—(m)—lion

Leonela—(f)—lion

Leonore—(f)—shining illumination, beacon, lightness, luminosity, radiance

Leonore—(m)—shining illumination, beacon, lightness, luminosity, radiance

Leopold—(m)—prince of the public, people, demos, folk, many

Leopolda—(f)—of the public, people, demos, folk, many

Leopoldine—(f)—of the public, people, demos, folk, many

Leroux—(m)—the red-haired one

Lewis—(m)—warrior

Liam—(m)—with the will as a powerful, strong, energetic

Liana—(f)—vine, to bind, young, juvenescent, under-age, youthful

Lianna—(f)—vine, to bind, young, juvenescent, under-age, youthful

Lien—(f)—lotus

Lies—(f)—deity has sworn

Liesbeth—(f)—deity has sworn

Lieselotte—(f)—combination name of elizabeth

Lieselotte—(f)—dear, darling, sweetheart by deity

Liliane—(f)—deity has sworn

Liliane—(f)—innocence, purity, beauty

Lina—(f)—derived from ending of carolina

Linda—(f)—shield of linden wood

Linde—(f)—shield of linden wood

Lindie—(f)—snake

Linn—(f)—linnet bird, flaxen

Lion—(m)—young lion

Lisa—(f)—deity has sworn

Lise—(f)—dedicated to deity

Livvy—(f)—olive tree

Livy—(f)—olive tree

Liz—(f)—deity's oath

Lizzy—(f)—deity's oath

Lodovico—(m)—noted, celebrated, shining, well-known, well-born warrior

Lorayne—(f)—place name

Lore—(f)—laurel wreath, crowned with laurel

Lorenzo—(m)—the award-winning

Loretta—(f)—where lothar dwells

Loring—(m)—warrior

Lorraine—(f)—warrior maiden

Lorrie—(f)—where lothar dwells

Lorry—(f)—where lothar dwells

Lotario—(m)—warrior

Lotte—(f)—masculine

Louis—(m)—noble, kingly, supreme, statuesque war hero, warrior

Louise—(f)—noble, kingly, supreme, statuesque war hero

Louisiana—(f)—warrior maiden

Lowell—(m)—young wolf

Luana—(f)—warrior maiden

Luc—(m)—from lucania, illumination, beacon, lightness, luminosity, radiance

Lucas—(m)—from lucania, illumination, beacon, lightness, luminosity, radiance

Lucile—(f)—illumination, beacon, lightness, luminosity, radiance

Lucrece—(f)—wealth, money, piles, rich, mammon

Ludo—(m)—noble, kingly, supreme, statuesque war hero

Ludwina—(f)—public, people, demos, folk, many

Lughaidh—(m)—noted, celebrated, shining, well-known, well-born fighter

Luisa—(f)—warrior maiden

Luka—(m)—from lucania, illumination, beacon, lightness, luminosity, radiance

Lukas—(m)—masculinity

Luna—(f)—deitydess of the moon

Lurleen—(f)—temptress

Lutgarde—(f)—public, people, demos, folk, many

Lynn—(f)—shield of linden wood, hose

Lyssa—(f)—gently born, truth

XIII

Belgian Baby Names—M

Maaike—(f)—shapely clean

Maarten—(m)—fondness of war

Maarten—(m)—the little warrior

Macey—(f)—gift, present, keepsake, fairing, bounty, prize of deity

Maddalen—(f)—magnificent

Maddy—(f)—female, woman, lady from magdala

Madelhari—(m)—war counsellor

Madelon—(f)—female, woman, lady from magdala

Madelon—(m)—female, woman, lady from magdala

Madie—(f)—tower

Magnhilda—(f)—powerful, strong, energetic, sledgehammer

Magnolia—(f)—flower

Maibelle—(f)—my fair maid, affection, dearness, devotion, mashly

Maite—(f)—dearly affection, dearness, devotion, mashd,

Majori—(f)—pearl
Mal—(f)—army counsellor
Malika—(f)—queen
Mallory—(f)—army counsellor
Mallory—(m)—war counselor
Malori—(f)—army counsellor
Manneville—(m)—from the great estate
Manon—(f)—shapely clean
Marc—(m)—son of mars
Marceau—(m)—deity of war
Marcello—(m)—deity of war
Marclyn—(f)—deity of war
Margaux—(f)—pearl
Margie—(f)—pearl
Margo—(f)—ornament, pearl
Margot—(f)—pearl
Margrit—(f)—pearl
Marian—(f)—despiteful, swart, sardonic
Mariann—(f)—little mary
Marie—(f)—shapely clean
Marieke—(f)—shapely clean
Mariele—(f)—despiteful, swart, sardonic
Marijke—(f)—shapely clean
Marilda—(f)—noted, celebrated, shining, well-born
battle, fight
Marina—(f)—shapely clean
Marjolein—(f)—maria+lina
Marjory—(f)—pearl
Marleen—(f)—shapely clean
Marlies—(f)—from the sea
Marlisa—(f)—despiteful, swart, sardonic
Marthe—(f)—the biblical figure marta
Martine—(f)—the little warrior

Masen—(m)—stone worker

Maslen—(m)—little twin

Mathias—(m)—keepsake, fairing, bounty, prize from deity

Mathieu—(m)—gift, present, keepsake, fairing, bounty

Mathieu—(m)—present, keepsake, fairing, bounty

Mathild—(f)—mighty battle, fight, fighting, war, action

Mats—(m)—deity's gift, present, keepsake, fairing, bounty, prize

Matthias—(m)—gift, present, keepsake, fairing, bounty, prize from deity

Maud—(f)—mighty in battle, fight, fighting, struggle

Maude—(f)—fight, fighting, war, action, struggle

Maurice—(m)—moor, an inhabitant of mauritania

Maxim—(m)—the largest

Maxime—(m)—the largest

Maya—(f)—mother

Mayne—(m)—powerful, strong, energetic, sledgehammer, driving

Meinke—(m)—firm, strong, steadfast, tenacious, resolute, determined

Melanie—(f)—black, dark, somber, dusky, unlit, ebon in color

Melissa—(f)—bee

Melodie—(f)—melody

Merel—(f)—blackbird

Merla—(f)—blackbird

Merlin—(m)—falcon

Merlyn—(f)—blackbird

Merrick—(m)—noted, celebrated, shining, well-known, well-born, of the sea

Meyer—(m)—farmer, peasant, husbandman, agriculturist, agriculturalist, swain

Michael—(m)—who is like a deity

Michel—(m)—who is like a deity

Michelle—(f)—who is like deity

Michiel—(m)—who is like a deity

Mieke—(f)—gracious, sweet and despiteful, smart, sardonic, sad

Miguel—(m)—who is like a deity

Mike—(m)—who is like a deity

Mikel—(m)—like a deity

Milan—(m)—affection, dearness, devotion, mash fame

Mili—(f)—industrious, strength

Milly—(f)—industrious, strength

Mindy—(f)—affection, dearness, devotion, mash

Miquel—(m)—like a deity

Mirla—(f)—blackbird

Monika—(f)—pretty, affection, dearness, devotion, handsome, scenic, grace

Monique—(f)—madonna, wise

Montgomery—(m)—mountain hunter

Myna—(f)—affection, dearness, devotion, mash

Myriam—(f)—marjoram

Myril—(m)—noted, celebrated, shining, well-known, well-born, of the sea

Myrthe—(f)—happiness and fertility

XIV

Belgian Baby Names—N

Nadia—(f)—hope

Nadine—(f)—hope

Nancy—(f)—favor, graciousness, indulgence

Nancy—(f)—favor, graciousness, indulgence of deity

Nannette—(f)—favor, graciousness, indulgence

Naomi—(f)—pleasurable, delicious, illumination, beacon, easeful

Natale—(m)—christmas

Natalee—(f)—born at christmas

Natasja—(f)—birthday of christ

Nathalia—(f)—born at christmas

Nathalie—(f)—birthday

Nathan—(m)—gift, present, keepsake, fairing, bounty, prize from deity

Natuche—(f)—born at christmas

Nele—(f)—the horned

Nelleke—(f)—horn

Nette—(f)—deity is gracious

Nev—(m)—new village

Nick—(m)—people, demos, folk, many, affection, dearness

Nico—(m)—conqueror of the public, people, demos, folk, many

Nicolas—(m)—people, demos, folk, many, affection, dearness, devotion

Niek—(m)—demos, folk, many, affection, dearness, devotion

Niels—(m)—the horned

Nikita—(f)—people, demos, folk, many, affection, dearness, devotion

Nikki—(f)—conqueror of the public, people, demos, folk, many

Nils—(m)—the horned

Nina—(f)—the ever holy, pure, sanctified, pious, solemn, chaste

Ninette—(f)—favor, graciousness, indulgence

Ninon—(f)—favor, graciousness, indulgence

Noa—(f)—movement

Noah—(m)—rust, comfort

Noelle—(f)—christmas

Noor—(f)—illumination, beacon, lightness, luminosity, radiance

Nora—(f)—deity is my illumination, beacon, lightness, luminosity, radiance

Norberaht—(f)—radiant, vivid, orient, splendent, flamboyant heroine

Norberta—(f)—blond hero

Norice—(m)—caretaker

Norman—(m)—from the north

Normie—(m)—from the north

XV

Belgian Baby Names—O

Oda—(f)—elfin spear

Odbart—(m)—one who is wealthy and rich

Odelina—(f)—elfin spear

Odila—(f)—elfin spear

Odo—(m)—name of bishop

Olinda—(f)—protector, defender, keeper, saviour, life saver, intercessor of property

Olivette—(f)—olive tree

Olivia—(f)—olive tree

Olivier—(m)—olive tree

Olley—(m)—olive tree

Olly—(f)—olive tree

Olly—(m)—olive tree

Olympe—(f)—from olympus

Omar—(m)—noted, celebrated, shining, well-known, well-born

Orane—(f)—rising

Ormand—(m)—serpent
Ormanda—(f)—of the sea
Orvalle—(m)—one from the golden village
Othmann—(m)—wealthy
Otilio—(m)—wealthy and fortunate person
Otthilde—(f)—fortunate heroine

XVI
Belgian Baby Names—P

Paige—(m)—young attendant

Pansy—(f)—flower

Pascal—(m)—born on easter

Pascal—(m)—easter, born on easter sunday

Pascali—(m)—born on easter

Pascaline—(f)—girl, gal, daughter, damsel born during easter

Pasclina—(f)—born at easter

Patricia—(f)—aristocrat

Patrick—(m)—gently bornman

Paul—(m)—small, modest

Paulien—(f)—small, low

Pauline—(f)—humble

Peer—(m)—rock form of peter

Peggy—(f)—variant of peg, diminutive of margaret

Peppi—(m)—petitioner

Perahta—(f)—noble, kingly, supreme, statuesque

Perren—(m)—rock, stone
Perryn—(m)—rock, stone
Peter—(m)—rock
Petra—(f)—rock
Petronille—(f)—rock
Philippe—(m)—horses friend
Phillipe—(m)—affection, dearness, devotion
Piercy—(m)—rock
Pierre—(m)—rock
Piers—(m)—rock
Pieter—(m)—rock
Pieterjan—(m)—rock
Plat—(m)—from the flat land, one belonging to the flat land
Porteur—(m)—gatekeeper, carrier
Portier—(m)—gatekeeper, carrier

XVII

Belgian Baby Names—Q

Quent—(m)—fifth-born child
Quentrell—(m)—fifth-born child
Quinten—(m)—fifth

XVIII
Belgian Baby Names—R

Raf—(m)—occurs in southern netherlands

Rainhard—(m)—powerful, strong, energetic, sledgehammer

Rald—(m)—noted, celebrated, shining, well-known, well-born leader

Rance—(m)—kind of belgian marble

Rani—(f)—song

Ranier—(m)—powerful, strong, energetic, sledgehammer, driving counsellor

Rayder—(m)— counsellor

Raylen—(m)— counsellor

Raymond—(m)—guards wisely

Rayner—(m)—wise warrior

Rebecca—(f)—wife of isaac and mother of jacob

Reeva—(f)—river

Reiner—(m)—counsel

Remy—(f)—from rheims

Renaud—(m)—valiant, gallant, heroic, daring, valorous one

Rene—(m)—reborn

Renne—(m)—to rise again

Renzo—(m)—masculinity

Rey—(m)—regal

Reynard—(m)—powerful, strong, energetic, sledgehammer, driving counsellor

Reynart—(m)—valiant, gallant, heroic, daring, valorous and powerful, strong

Ria—(f)—river

Ricard—(m)—powerful ruler

Rick—(m)—powerful ruler

Rickard—(m)—powerful ruler

Ricker—(m)—powerful ruler

Ricky—(f)—powerful ruler

Ricky—(m)—powerful ruler

Rik—(m)—ruler king

Rikkert—(m)—powerful ruler

Rillie—(f)—brook

Ringling—(m)—ring

Riocard—(m)—powerful ruler

Rita—(f)—shapely clean

Rive—(f)—river

Rob—(m)—pretty, affection, dearness, devotion, handsome

Robb—(m)—radiant, vivid, orient, splendent, flamboyant, noted

Robbe—(m)—pretty, affection, dearness, devotion, handsome, scenic

Robby—(m)—pretty, affection, dearness, devotion, handsome

Robert—(m)—radiant, vivid, orient, splendent, flamboyant with glory

Robin—(m)—pretty, affection, dearness, devotion, handsome, scenic

Robinette—(f)—small robin

Roch—(m)—glory

Rochette—(f)—from the little rock

Rodel—(m)—noted, celebrated, shining, well-known, well-born ruler

Rodgers—(m)—noted, celebrated, shining, well-known, well-born spearman

Rodrik—(m)—noted, shining, well-known, well-born ruler

Roel—(m)—noted, celebrated, shining, well-known, well-born in the country

Roeland—(m)—noted, celebrated, shining, well-known

Roger—(m)—noted, celebrated, shining, well-known

Roland—(m)—noted, celebrated, shining, well-known

Rolanda—(f)—celebrated, shining, well-known

Romana—(f)—from rome

Romhilda—(f)—noble, kingly, supreme

Romy—(f)—rosemary, person from rome

Roosevelt—(m)—field of roses

Rosalind—(f)—little red-haired one

Rosamonde—(f)—rose

Rosemaria—(f)—despiteful, swart, sardonic

Rosemonde—(f)—defender, keeper, saviour, life saver, intercessor

Rosey—(m)—field of roses

Rosie—(m)—field of roses

Rosselin—(f)—little red-haired one

Rossiter—(m)—red surname

Roth—(m)—red-haired

Rousse—(m)—red-haired

Rowland—(m)—noted, celebrated, shining, well-known, well-born soldier

Roxane—(f)—dawn

Roy—(m)—king, regal

Royale—(m)—gently born one

Ruben—(m)— beholden

Rudella—(f)—noted, celebrated, shining, well-known

Rudi—(m)—famed wolf

Rudy—(m)—famed wolf, wolf

Rune—(m)—secret lore

Ruprecht—(m)—radiant, vivid, orient, splendent, flamboyant, noted, celebrated

Russ—(m)—red-haired

Russel—(m)—red-haired

Ruth—(f)—companion, friend

XIX

Belgian Baby Names—S

Sabine—(f)—of the tribe of the sabines, from sabine, italy

Sabrina—(f)—legendary princess

Sam—(f)—diminutive of samson, sun child, radiant, vivid, orient

Sam—(m)—diminutive of samson, sun child, radiant, vivid

Sander—(m)—protector, defender, keeper, saviour, life saver, intercessor of men

Sandra—(f)—unheeded prophetess

Sanne—(f)—lily

Sara—(f)—princess

Sarah—(f)—princess

Saskia—(f)—protector, defender, keeper, savior, life saver, intercessor of humanity

Sauville—(m)—from the willow farm

Schuyler—(f)—shield, scholar

Schuyler—(m)—shield, scholar

Searle—(m)—manly

Selda—(f)—noted, celebrated, shining, well-known, well-born warrior

Selik—(m)—blessed

Selina—(f)—variant of celine

Selma—(f)—divine, providential, supernal protector

Senne—(m)—majestic

Seppe—(m)—victory, conquest, success, victory, conquest, success

Serge—(m)—servant

Serilda—(f)—armed maiden of war

Seton—(m)—from baron's estate

Sevrin—(m)—strict, restrained

Shana—(f)—deity is gracious

Shantay—(f)—enchanted

Shauni—(f)—deity is gracious

Shauny—(f)—deity is with us

Sherry—(f)—dear, darling, sweetheart, dear

Sibyla—(f)—prophetess

Sid—(f)—from the city of st. **D**enis

Sidoney—(f)—from the city of st. **D**enis

Siebe—(m)—victory, conquest, success

Sien—(f)—frenchman

Sigfreda—(f)—victorious

Sigourney—(f)—daring king

Silke—(f)—win

Silvestre—(m)—trees, sylvan

Simon—(m)—deity has heard

Sky—(f)—shield, scholar

Sky—(m)—shield, scholar

Skye—(f)—shield, scholar

Skye—(m)—shield, scholar

Skylar—(f)—shield, scholar

Skylar—(m)—shield, scholar
Skyler—(f)—shield, scholar
Skyler—(m)—shield, scholar
Slania—(f)—health and wellness
Sofie—(f)—intelligence, sagacity, dexterity, sobering, sapience
Solaina—(f)—arrogant, conceited, haughty, proud, pretentious
Sonja—(f)—intelligence, sagacity, dexterity, sobering, sapience
Sonnenschein—(f)—sunshine
Spangler—(m)—tinsmith
Stef—(m)—crown, garland
Stefaan—(m)—crown, garland
Stefania—(f)—crowned in victory, conquest, success
Stefanie—(f)—crown
Steinmetz—(m)—stonemason, stone
Stephanie—(f)—crown, wreath
Steve—(m)—wreath
Steven—(m)—crown, wreath
Stijn—(m)—stone weapon
Stine—(m)—stone
Suzanne—(f)—lily
Sven—(m)—boy, young man
Sylvia—(f)—forest, wood, bush
Sylvie—(f)—from the forest, wood, bush

XX

Belgian Baby Names—T

Tahbert—(m)—brilliant

Talbot—(m)—bloodhound

Tamara—(f)—palm tree

Tatiana—(f)—unknown

Taylor—(m)—tailor

Tearlach—(m)—manly

Tess—(f)—harvester

Tessa—(f)—female, lady lady working at harvest

Theo—(m)—the boldest

Theon—(m)—untamed

Thibault—(m)—valiant, gallant, heroic, daring, valorous

Thibaut—(m)—valiant, gallant, heroic, daring, valorous among the public

Thijs—(m)—name from the new testament

Thomas—(m)—twin

Thrisha—(f)—intellectual

Tibo—(m)—public, people, demos, folk, many

Tifany—(f)—appearance of deity

Tiff—(f)—appearance of deity

Tiffany—(f)—appearance of deity

Tiffy—(f)—appearance of deity

Tille—(f)—strength in battle, fight, fighting, war, action, struggle

Tim—(m)—short version of timotheus

Timothy—(m)—one who honours the deity

Tina—(f)—deity has sworn

Tine—(f)—follower, henchman, disciple, sectary

Tom—(m)—twin

Tommy—(m)—twin

Toon—(m)—invaluable

Tretan—(m)—walks

Trever—(m)—crossing

Tristan—(m)—tumult, outcry

Tristian—(m)—outcry

Troilus—(m)—place name

Troilus—(m)—son of priam

Trude—(f)—from gertrude

Tryne—(f)—holy, pure, sanctified, pious, solemn, chaste

XXI

Belgian Baby Names—U

Udolf—(m)—wolf ruler
Uli—(f)—mistress of all
Uli—(m)—gently born leader
Ulva—(f)—wolf
Ulz—(m)—gently born leader
Unna—(f)—female, lady dona

XXII

Belgian Baby Names—V

Valeray—(m)—valiant, gallant, heroic, daring, valorous

Valere—(f)—valiant, gallant, heroic, daring, valorous

Valerie—(f)—powerful, strong, energetic, sledgehammer

Valery—(f)—valiant, gallant, heroic, daring, valorous

Vallerie—(f)—valiant, gallant, heroic, daring, valorous

Vallois—(m)—welshman

Vanessa—(f)—butterfly

Vanya—(f)—gracious, female, woman, lady who is favour, graciousness

Vayle—(m)—from the vale

Veerle—(f)—battle, fight, fighting, war, action

Vera—(f)—belief, faith, affiance, assurance, credence, sureness

Verddun—(m)—from the green hill

Verena—(f)—protector, defender, keeper, saviour, life saver, intercessor

Verner—(m)—defending the army

Veronique—(f)—bringing victory, conquest, success

Verrill—(m)—real, true, accurate, precise, exact, actual

Viau—(m)—intense, acute, rapid, fast, sharp, lively

Vicky—(f)—victor

Vidal—(m)—life, existence, lifemanship

Vignetta—(f)—little vine

Vince—(m)—victor, conqueror, vanquisher, victress, subjugator, king-of-arms

Vincent—(m)—win, vanquish, conquer, surmount, pull off, subjugate

Virginie—(f)—holy, pure, sanctified, pious, solemn, chaste, virgin

Viviane—(f)—lively, full of life

XXIII

Belgian Baby Names—W

Wagner—(m)—wagon driver

Walborgd—(f)—protecting ruler

Waldemar—(m)—noted, celebrated, shining, well-known, well-born ruler

Waldo—(m)—divine, providential, super powerful

Walt—(m)—powerful ruler

Walter—(m)—ruler of the army

Wandis—(f)—wanderer

Wannes—(m)—yahweh is gracious

Ward—(m)—wealth, patron, guardian, custodian, protector, trustee

Wareine—(m)—patron, guardian, custodian, protector, trustee, promoter

Warre—(m)—guardian, custodian, protector, trustee, promoter of the property

Weber—(m)—weaver

Welda—(f)—ruler, king, governor, lord, duke, chief

Wendy—(f)—literary

Wesley—(m)—from the west meadow

Wesley—(m)—the west meadow

Wiatt—(m)—guide, manual, cicerone, road book, enchiridion

Wietse—(m)—wide, far

Wilde—(f)—untamed

Wilhelm—(m)—german form of william

Willard—(m)—bold, resolute

Willem—(m)—with the will as powerful, strong, energetic, sledgehammer

William—(m)—energetic, sledgehammer, driving ashelmet

Willy—(m)—with the will as powerful, strong, energetic, sledgehammer, swingeing

Wilmer—(m)—resolute, noted, celebrated, shining, well-known, well-born

Wilmet—(f)—protector, defender, keeper, saviour, life saver, intercessor

Wim—(m)—determined protector, defender, keeper, saviour, life saver, intercessor

Wolfric—(m)—wolf ruler

Wout—(m)—ruler of the army

Wouter—(m)—ruler of the army

XXIV

Belgian Baby Names—X

Belgian Baby Names—X

Xander—(m)—protector, defender, keeper, saviour, life saver, intercessor of men

Xavier—(m)—illumination, beacon, lightness, luminosity

Yana—(f)—deity is reconciling

Yannick—(m)—yahweh is gracious

Yara—(f)—spring

Yaro—(m)—descendant, scion, offspring, progeny, son, child

Yasmine—(f)—jasmine blossom

Yoni—(f)—yahweh is gracious

Yorben—(m)—bear with the spear

Yves—(m)—the archer

Zelda—(f)—noted, celebrated, shining, well-known, well-born warrior

Zelinda—(f)—shield of victory, conquest, success

Zita—(f)—girl, gal, daughter, damsel

Zurie—(f)—white and affection, dearness, devotion, mashly

****

****

www.ingramcontent.com/pod-product-compliance
Lightning Source LLC
Chambersburg PA
CBHW022100150726
47990CB00003B/1183